The Fisherman's Catch

A Conservative Bedtime Story

Written By Thomas Wright	Illustrated by Heather Dixon

" There is no such thing as a good tax. "

- Sir Winston Churchill

"The power to tax is the power to destroy."

- Chief Justice John Marshall in McCulloch v. Maryland

This book is dedicated to my wife and kids
for your love and help
-Thomas Wright

Copyright © 2010 by Ivory Dusk L.C.
All rights reserved.

Published By Ivory Dusk L.C.

No Part of this publication may be reproduced in whole or in part, stored in a retrieval system, or transmitted in any form or by any means, electronic, mechanical, photocopying, recording, or otherwise, without the written permission of the publisher.

For information regarding permission, email to admin@ConservativeBedtimeStories.com subject line: Permissions.

Printed in the United States by BookMasters, Inc.,
30 Amberwood Parkway, Ashland, Ohio 44805, May, 2010
Job # M7326

First Edition - May 2010

ISBN 10 : 0-98270990-0
ISBN 13 : 978-0-98270990-0

Once upon a time, in a far away land, on a far away island, there lived a fisherman named Hanauhoulani, or more simply, Han. Han used a spear to catch fish in the vast ocean.

He would spend all day long fishing but only bring in a few fish.

One day Han noticed a spider catching flies in her web. He was impressed that the clever spider did not have to hunt for the flies. Instead, she patiently waited for them to get caught.

Maybe I can make a web for fish, thought Han.

Han was determined to make a web.

He fished by day and worked on his web by night.

He made many mistakes, but he did not give up.

After a year of hard work, Han had finally made a web!

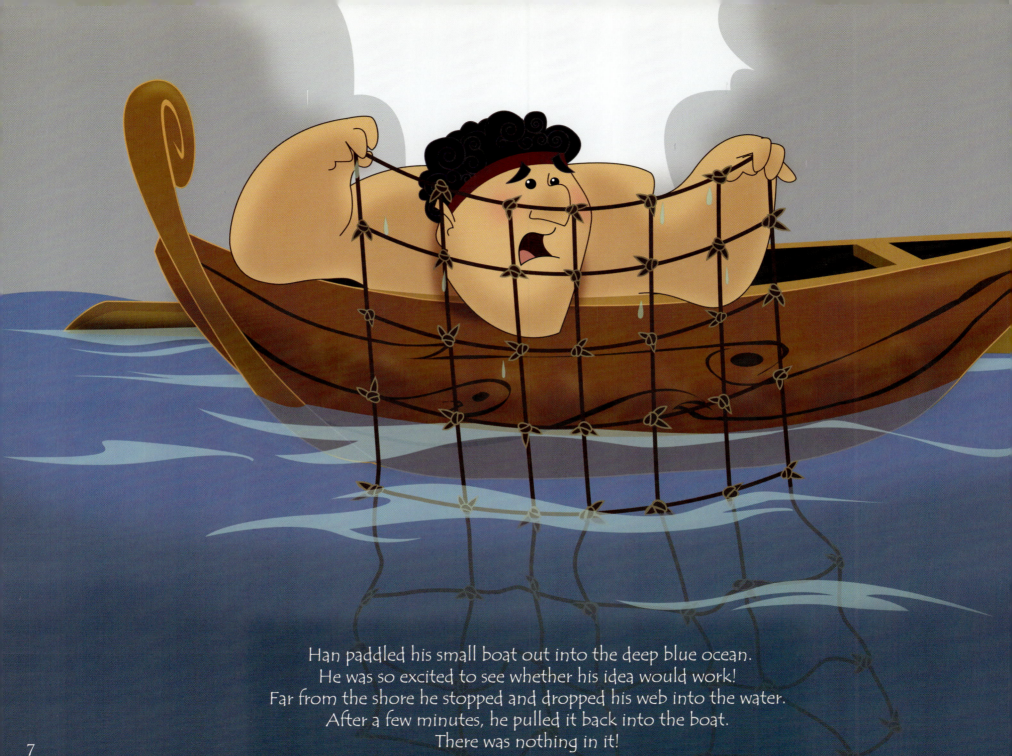

Han paddled his small boat out into the deep blue ocean.
He was so excited to see whether his idea would work!
Far from the shore he stopped and dropped his web into the water.
After a few minutes, he pulled it back into the boat.
There was nothing in it!

Tired and sad, Han paddled back toward the shore.
However, the more he paddled,
the slower his little boat went.
Looking around for the reason, he noticed
that his web was caught on part of the boat.
Curious, Han tugged on the web.

It barely moved!

It was filled with all kinds of fish!

When Han returned home, the villagers were delighted to see so many fish! Since his catch was so large, Han decided he did not need as much in trade for each fish. Even the poorest villager could afford some now!
Everyone was happy…

Well, almost everyone.

Bera, the village chief, noticed not only that some people could not afford Han's fish as often as others, but that Han himself was becoming wealthy.

It is not fair for one man to have so much while others have so much less, thought Bera.

Bera called his men together and went to see Han. He explained to Han that they were going to take half of his catch each day for "the good of the village". Han protested, "I don't think it is right for you to take something that is not yours."

Bera was upset. "I am the chief," he reminded Han. "I know what is right for the village!" Bera then told his men to push Han aside and take half the fish back to the village.

From that day on, Bera gave Han's fish to the poor of the village. At first only the sick and truly needy were given fish, but after a short time, other villagers figured out that Bera would give fish to them if they stopped working.

"Why should we work when we can have fish handed to us?" they reasoned.

As more people needed help,
Bera took even more fish from Han.

Not all of the villagers liked what the chief was doing to Han. Many of the farmers, hunters, and other workers grew worried.

If Han can have his fish taken, then what will stop Bera from taking our things away, they wondered.

Bera noticed that despite the fish he gave to the needy villagers, they always seemed to need more. It also seemed that regardless of how many fish Bera took from Han, Han was still much more wealthy than they were.

Bera took more and more fish from Han to give to the poor.

After all, thought Bera, *Han still has so much more than he needs.*

One day, the merchant who had traded rope and twine to Han stopped by the village. He arrived just in time to see Bera and his men pull a cart away with most of Han's catch. The merchant asked, "Why are they taking your fish away?" Han sadly told the merchant what had happened.

"I have an idea," said the merchant. "We need a fisherman in our village and would love to have you live with us."

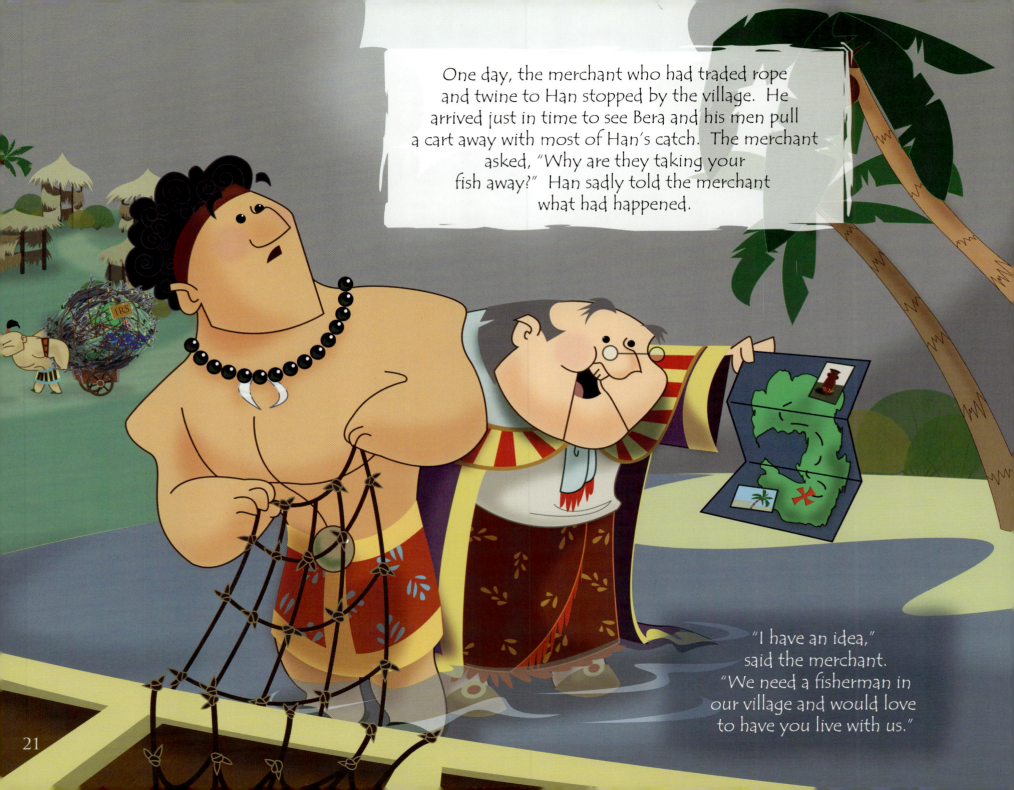

The merchant promised Han that his village would not take away any of his catch. They would simply be happy to trade for the fish. Han decided to go with the merchant to start a new life.

Bera came by the next day for fish, but Han's house was empty. He looked through the village; he went out to the shore. He wondered, *where could Han be?* He returned to the village with no fish.
Many of the villagers were angry.

It was then Bera realized that there were others in the village with more than they needed. He could take from them to give to the less fortunate! Bera started taking from those that still worked and gave their things to the poor villagers.

This made the people who worked angry!

They had struggled and sacrificed to grow the food and create the things that Bera was simply taking from them.

One by one, they too decided to leave.

Bera did not understand how his village had become a bad place to live. He thought that by taking from those with plenty and giving to those in need, he was making things fair for everyone.

Soon Bera's Village became deserted.

Meanwhile, the people in the merchant's village were thankful Han had joined them. They liked to watch as he went out in his boat to catch fish.

Han became very wealthy, but felt that he should be generous with his wealth and his knowledge.
He helped others achieve their own ideas and dreams.

Han's new village became known as a place of hard work and great wealth. It became a land of opportunity. People came there to try to live a better life. Because of their hard work, Han and the people in the merchant's village--

Inspired by Han, farmers thought of new ways to grow crops. Hunters came up with new ideas to catch animals. Weavers tried new methods to create baskets. Not every idea was successful, but some were.

-- lived very, very, happily ever after.

Questions:

Have you ever had a good idea? Did it work the first time you tried it?

Why were the fish less expensive when Han was able to catch more at once?

How did you feel when Bera took Han's fish?

Can trying to make something fair have the opposite effect? Explain.

Did giving fish to the poor make them less poor?
Where does real wealth come from?

There is a saying, "You can give a person a fish and feed him for a day, or teach that person to fish and feed them everyday." What does it mean?

Was Bera trying to be a good person?

Is there a difference between Han giving his fish to the poor and Bera taking the fish from Han to give to the poor? Why is that difference important?

What do you think the story meant when it said the merchant's village became a land of opportunity? Did it mean everyone was rich? Why is opportunity important?

Is it important to be generous? Why?

In Depth questions for Advanced Thinkers:

Did the wealth of Bera's village increase as Han's productivity increased? Explain the concept behind that and how it could be applied to our world.

Wealth is relative. If you were to compare Han's wealth (what he possessed) with your own, was he really all that wealthy? Why is the relativity of wealth an important concept to understand?

"The End Justifies the Means" is used when trying to explain why hurting one person or group of people is okay, if in the end it helps more people as a result. Bera took Han's fish without compensation and gave them to others. Why is the method used as important as the result it achieves? What other ways could Bera have helped people without taking from Han?

Taxation is sometimes viewed as a necessary evil. The Government needs to be able to pay for things such as roads and civil protection. Is it possible to distinguish between a vital government program and a program that is simply socially popular (like getting free fish in the story)? What should a government's role be in social responsibility?

Because of Bera's government program, the people in his village became dependent on Han. Once Han left, rather than dismantling the government program, Bera simply passed the cost onto others. Where can this be seen in our current government programs? Is it a problem?

Often times a government program is set up with a limited purpose. Bera started off by giving a few fish to people who were very poor. Very quickly the program grew larger and he needed to take more from the fisherman. Does this happen with other government programs? If so, why?

How is the idea of generosity and giving of one's own wealth for a good cause different from one being forced to give in order to do the same good?